Medical to Mystical

Bring Light into Your Life

Dr. Susan Jamieson M.D.

f

FINDHORN PRESS

First published in 2008 by AuthorHouse UK Ltd.
This edition published in 2010 by Findhorn Press, Scotland

ISBN 978-1-84409-193-5

Printed and bound in the European Union

1 2 3 4 5 6 7 8 9 10 11 12 13 14 15 14 13 12 11 10

Published by
Findhorn Press
305a The Park, Findhorn
Forres IV36 3TE, Scotland, UK
t +44-(0)1309-690582
f +44-(0)131-777-2177
e info@findhornpress.com
www.findhornpress.com

Dedicated to my late mother, Averil,
who is still the brightest light in my life.

CONTENTS

comes from light. Physicists tell us that at the sub-atomic level we are made up of solid light. Recently we have found that our DNA emits light, as does our heart and the planet in which we live.

Colour is the part of the electromagnetic spectrum that we can see. We live in a world of colour. Everything we see in nature, the food we eat and clothes we wear are part of the light spectrum. It is the colour pigment in plants that makes up chemicals with health-giving properties such as anti-oxidants. This is so important because if we are truly beings of light, then we must be affected on a deep level by the light around us in all its forms, including colour. We are also affected by the form of other electromagnetic (light) forces, which can come from the hands of a healer or the electromagnetic emissions from the planet, or sun. We are surrounded!

This realization that everything is made of light has ramifications. If we and our environment are made of the same substance, it makes sense to be in harmony with each other and with nature.

This book explains how these light energies occur and how to access them in order to connect to our hidden resources.

Author's Note

TO ME, LIGHT IS everything. It's that all-pervading ground substance of the Universe; it's the energy of love; it's the light of God; it's the primordial mass from which we arose and it's that which connects us all in its shimmering web. It's my mission to help people understand the practical and fundamental concepts behind these ideas, so they can absorb, hold and share as much light as possible in this world in preparation for the next stage in human evolution.

Thousands of years ago, indigenous societies worldwide recognized our innate connection to the Earth, Sun and forces of nature outside our control. They embraced this concept and respected their environment and the planet, fully realizing their dependence on it for sustenance and survival.

I live in Hong Kong, meaning the 'Fragrant Harbour'. It sits at the gateway to China, Zhong Guo, which means 'Middle Kingdom', indicating that China is at the centre of the world. It's also in keeping with the ancient Qigong concept that man is in the middle, between Heaven and Earth, and literally a conduit between the two.

We in modern society have somehow lost this connection and awareness that we are one with nature. This sense of separateness is the cause of the many problems we have today. The misperception that others are essentially different from ourselves leads to abuses, cruelty, wars and genocide. Extending the same attitude to our planet allows for neglect and abuse of the Earth in all the ways we see happening today.

Before we're able to heal the planet, we must heal ourselves, and change our limited scope of perception, or misperceptions. As rationalizing beings, people need to understand the reasons behind any change of thinking or ways of being. This is all part of the indigenous healing tradition, which taught of the interconnectedness of all things. This knowledge and healing will produce a ripple effect which grows and grows until finally, when a critical mass is reached, there's a tsunami, of light.

"The word enlightenment conjures up the idea of some superhuman accomplishment, and the ego likes to keep it that way, but it is simply the natural state of felt oneness with Being. It is a state of connectedness with something immeasurable and indestructible, something that, almost paradoxically, is essentially you and yet is much greater than you. It is finding your true nature beyond name and form… the light is not separate from who you are but constitutes your very essence."

—Eckhart Tolle

"What if one were to run
after a ray of light?
What if one were riding on
the beam?"
—**Albert Einstein**

Chapter 1

Journey into the Light

I STOOD IN THE 55 degree Centigrade heat of the desert at Abu Simbel, Egypt, before the immense statues of Rameses II, the 19th dynasty pharaoh who ruled at the height of the Egyptian empire. The dazzling effect of the sun as it blazed down on the huge honey-coloured edifice was intensified by reflection off the surrounding sand and water. I had to stop, awed and dizzy, to rest on a stone, absorbing and integrating this new and powerful energy.

Something about the light around the monolith drew me on to investigating Rameses' forebear, Akhenaten, a light worshipper who was married to the beautiful Nefertiti. I became fascinated by this amazing pair who ruled the most sophisticated kingdom in 1300 B.C., in the golden age of the Egyptian empire. Over the period of their reign, the glamorous couple completely upset the status quo by overturning the long-held belief system in the many gods of ancient Egypt. The pharaoh Akhenaten and Nefertiti bravely started a brand new religion, worshipping the light, making its source, the sun, or Aten, the new God of ancient Egypt.

Rejecting all myths and symbols along with the many other gods of ancient Egypt, for the first time in history, one god only was worshipped — this was monotheism 500 years ahead of the birth of Judaism. Akhenaten had found a direct path from the human to the divine in worshipping light, the one Universal God.

For me, this Egyptian experience led to newfound insights and knowledge which increasingly integrated the practical medical school-learnt skills of being a physician, with my nature, one of a mystic. Through my work as a doctor, it was becoming apparent to me that light itself was incredibly special and powerful. I knew intuitively that light was both the fabric and the connecting substance of everything — the 'ground substance' of the Universe discussed by physicists. As a family doctor for many years in the UK and Hong Kong I had begun to notice something unusual about my patients.

"From within or from behind, a light shines through us upon things, and makes us aware that we are nothing, but the light is all."
—Ralph Waldo Emerson

'I found that I could instantly recognize any who were depressed the moment they walked into the room.'

It wasn't anything to do with their body language, rather some indefinable property. For some reason, this was most obvious in cases of depression or anxiety, where the mood would be strong enough to colour their energy in an obvious way.

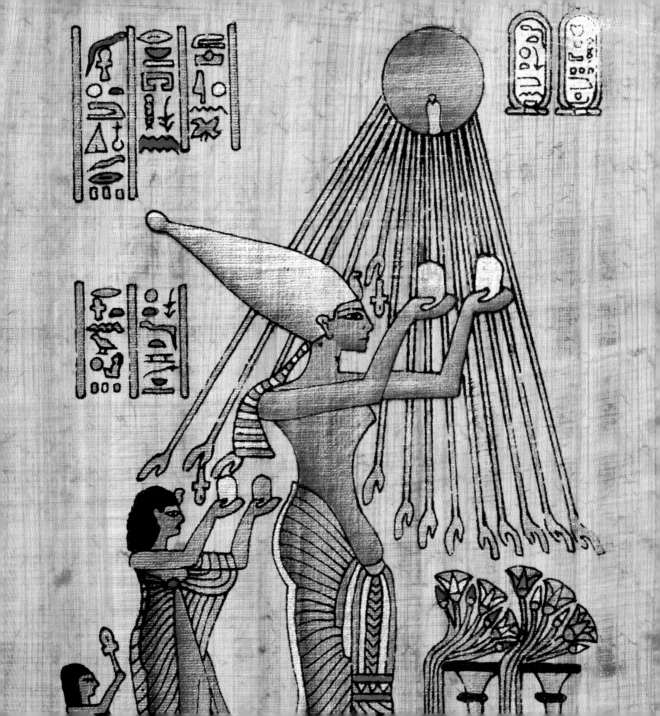

However, soon I began to notice this difference in anyone seriously ill. In comparison to other patients, perhaps pregnant women, most children, or those who wanted check-ups, these sick patients had a different quality of energy about them.

'After some time it came to me that the difference was in their "light".'

A person's light took on different qualities, depending on the nature of their illness or problems. Their light could be fresh and translucent, like shafts of sunlight filtering through the vibrant green leaves of a tree. In most illness the light is not clear and flowing freely, 'stagnant Qi', as the Chinese would say. It might be murky like a polluted pond, dully reflecting the clarity of nature in its surroundings. The light may be obscured by a mouldy growth, only allowing patches to filter down into the water. Or like a dirty car windscreen, with streaks of light distorted through the glass. The other side of the coin, I noted when I was in the presence of someone considered to be 'enlightened'.

'For example, the modern spiritual philosopher Eckhart Tolle, author of books such as "The Power of Now".'

Attending one of his workshops a few years ago I noticed he literally appeared to radiate light around him, like a whole body halo. At the end

"Whenever you are present, you become 'transparent' to some extent to the light, the pure consciousness that emanates from this Source. You also realize that the light is not separate from who you are but constitutes your very essence."
—Eckhart Tolle

of these functions it's his habit to hug members of the audience. All I was aware of at this time was that light emanated from him, becoming stronger when I touched him, and feeling rather uncomfortable as it appeared to expose any areas of darkness inside me. There was nowhere to hide in the light!

'Later, I learnt in my meditations
to connect with this special energy of the Sun's light.'

I can only describe my revelation as a feeling that I'm composed of small particles of shimmering light. Sometimes it seems as though I'm vibrating at a high frequency, when I feel as light as a feather, vibrant as a sunbeam. My energy is high and pure, able to lighten the darkest corners. In this higher vibration state, I am able to transcend any difficulty. Becoming this light, I have completely merged with the energy of my soul, I have the clear vision of an owl, along with the knowingness and wisdom of all that I am, ever have been and could be.

'I'm not always in this state and need to practise.
In the following chapters, I will share my knowledge and practice with you.
Then you'll know how to create and fulfil your own potential,
by absorbing, holding and sharing all the light that you can.'

Chapter 2

Light Science

AKHENATEN, THE EGYPTIAN PHARAOH, tried to explain the whole Universe on the basis of a single principle — light. However we had to wait for Einstein for light to be considered as an absolute reference point.

Einstein's General Theory of Relativity was based on his light theories, and as a youth, fascinated by light, he wondered, 'What if one were to run after a ray of light? What if one were riding on the beam?'

Physicists tell us that our bodies are made up of shimmering particles, moving in and out of perception so quickly that our eyes can't see them. Rather like a TV picture which is made up of oscillating photons — small particles of light — coming and going, like the tiny pinpricks of light on the screen. However, when we look at the TV screen, objects such as trees or dogs appear solid. Our senses just aren't quick enough to perceive this reality, in the same way that we perceive ourselves to be standing still in the world, yet the Earth orbits the sun at 30 km/sec whilst the whole solar system moves round the Milky Way at 250 km/sec.

'So, we are not solid. We're made of light particles, or electromagnetic (EM) energy. Einstein told us many years ago that $E=mc^2$ — energy is matter (multiplied by the speed of light squared). Therefore matter, such as our bodies, is energy. There is no difference, no separation. The physicist David Bohm considered matter to be "frozen light". Our bodies are light or electromagnetic (EM) energy and, as will be shown later in this book, also emitters and receivers of EM energy.'

Less scientifically, this is confirmed by people who experience 'near death', that is who are medically certified to be dead after an accident, then revive and generally tell a similar story. One of these is that when out of their bodies 'on the other side', they then perceived our world to be strangely unreal and flimsy, much less solid than it appears to us.

The electromagnetic spectrum comprises, amongst others, x-rays ultrasound and visible light colours, differentiated by their speed (frequency) and size (wavelength).

The basic unit of electromagnetic energy is the photon. Photons have no electrical charge, no mass (weight), and travel at the speed of light in a vacuum.

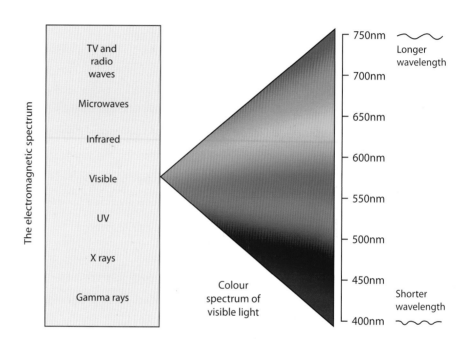

According to Einstein, time stops at the speed of light, therefore photons have no time either. Photons also manage to be two things at once, depending on their situation and also on how they're observed. They can be individual particles, or they can be a wave. They owe a lot of their extraordinary properties to the fact that they can multi-task in this way.

Light in biology

As biological beings, all our energy comes from our food. Whether we eat meat — animals thriving on plants (grass) — or fish — sustained by tiny algae organisms in the sea — birds, fruit or vegetables, the basic source of our nutrition is plants. We understand this through the process of photosynthesis.

'Photosynthesis:

Plants can convert energy from the Sun, in the form of light, to electrical then chemical energy, which we can then use as food. Light is the plants' food. This light to food energy conversion occurs in chlorophyll, the green pigment that colours vegetables. As all our food is derived from plants, it follows that by ingesting plants, we are also made of light.'

"Notice how present a flower is, how surrendered to life."
—Eckhart Tolle

Over the centuries, many scientists had speculated that cells contained light energy: Scottish physicist James Clerk Maxwell proposed in the 1800s that light consisted of a vibrating EM field.

The Russian scientist Lakhovsky's fundamental principle in 1925 was that every living thing emitted radiation. Albert Nodon in France proved this hypothesis, by showing that all living animals and plants emit radiation.

'He even found that, weight for weight, the radiation from certain flies, beetles and spiders, was up to 15 times that of uranium.'

In the 1970s, Fritz Popp, working in the Max Plank Institute of Astronomy in Heidelberg, Germany, showed that rapid growth in plants was associated with stronger light emissions, which would reduce as the plants aged. He also observed that when the cells died, they gave off a burst of light that had been stored somewhere inside them. The plant light emissions were called biophotons.

'Light in the body is thought to carry the information, or instructions, involved in triggering all biochemical reactions in our cells.'

Biologists have discovered that at the cellular level, all the enzyme systems (chemicals that make things work) in our body are activated by light messages. DNA is not the only light-reactive substance: the haem molecule, in haemoglobin, carries oxygen in our blood, and therefore circulates all round the body, and is an important example.[1]

Also light-reactive are the neurotransmitters of the brain, which regulate our moods. (Everyone has heard of the neurotransmitter serotonin, levels of which are raised by taking antidepressants such as

Prozac.) Another clinical example of our reaction to light is Seasonal Affective Disorder (SAD), a type of depression and fatigue especially common in countries with very short daylight hours in winter, such as those in Scandinavia. It's been found that exposing these patients to light therapy, using small portable light boxes, helps them tremendously.

Light therapy is also used to treat jet-lag, as light inhibits the brain's production of melatonin, which induces sleep. Light in the form of natural sunlight works best for this.

Light in DNA

It's been discovered that in human bodies, the origin of this light emission is DNA. So the most basic structure in our cells — our blueprint — release light.

'It's likely that our DNA act like a radio antenna, to receive and emit light.'

We now know that light is both stored and released from the DNA in every cell in our body. As we know, DNA make up our genes, which give us our unique properties and are capable of changing our physiology.

DNA — superconductor of light

In the 1990s, Dr Vladimir Poponin, quantum biologist at the Russian Academy of Science, discovered the DNA phantom effect. His experiments suggested that our DNA directly affect the physical world.

He clearly showed that if human DNA were added to a vacuum through which laser light was shone, the laser light would change its pattern so that it clustered round the DNA helix, in spirals.

The DNA had somehow affected the energy of the light photons. Even when the actual DNA sample was removed, the light would maintain the spiral shape — a phantom DNA. Even the energy of the DNA had affected the light pattern!

'This research suggests that there's a subtle energy related to DNA that reacts with standard EM energy, such as light.'

This phantom DNA theory could perhaps explain previously unexplained phenomena such as phantom limbs — this is when a person feels an itch, cramp or pain in a limb which has been amputated. Many years later, their brain is telling them that the limb is still present.

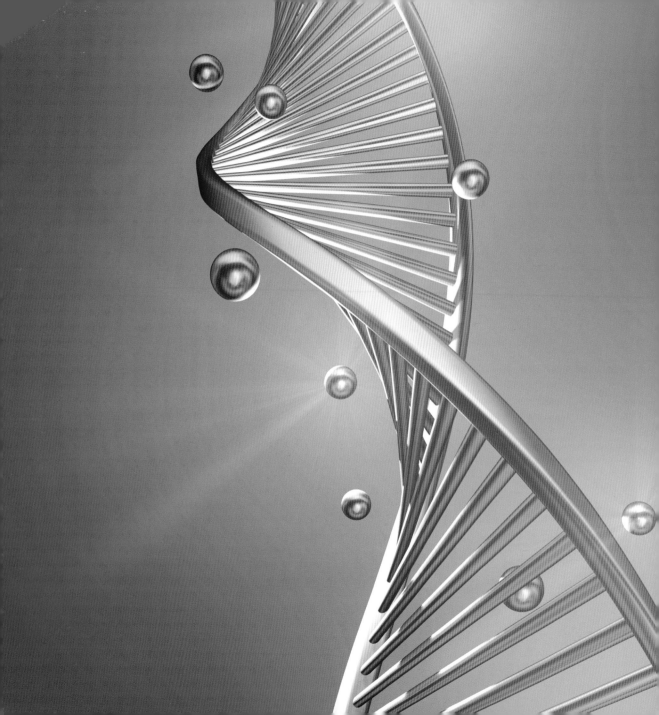

Similarly the phantom leaf effect — if a Kirlian photograph is taken of the plant's EM energy, it's found that even after cutting a leaf off a branch, that same leaf will still show up on the photograph of the branch. It's as though the branch had a memory of its EM energy wholeness.

'So, it's an empowering thought to accept that our DNA can affect the energy around us. We know from $E=mc^2$ that energy equals matter. Perhaps by connecting to this light in our DNA we can then manifest the world that we desire.'

> "All living things, including the Earth, radiate electromagnetic energy."

Chapter 3

Colour, a Frequency of Light

THE PART OF ELECTROMAGNETIC energy that we can see, of course, is the visible light/colour spectrum: red-orange-yellow-green-blue-indigo-violet. The other parts of the spectrum, such as ultraviolet, infrared and x-rays, may affect us, but we're not so aware of it at the time.

Colour in science and physiology

The significance of different colour frequencies can be seen from Einstein's photoelectric effect, for which he was awarded the Nobel Prize for physics in 1921. Even though the light photons have no mass they were shown to cause an electrical current when hitting a metal plate. The production of the current was dependent not on the quantity of light photons, but on the colour — frequency — of the photons. (Higher, e.g. blue, frequencies would cause a greater effect than red.) Apparently, in science the different colours are more important than we think.

'In fact, starting in the 1950s, researchers experimented
with the effects of colour on our physiology.'

Both the Russians and Americans found that, for example, red excited our autonomic nervous system. This is the part of our nervous system that, unlike our arm muscles, is not under conscious control. Examples would be the muscles of our respiratory system and gut, which work all day and night without us giving them instructions. So while the red colour would increase blood pressure and breathing rate, different colours such as blue calmed it (lowering pulse, sweating and respiratory rate).

Since then numerous experiments have been done on the connection between our health and light, including the use of red light to stop migraines and pink light in reducing muscle strength. The pink was found to be useful information in, for example, wall colours in prisons, where it helped reduce the tendency towards violence.

Blue light was discovered to cure jaundice in premature babies in the 1960s, a huge medical breakthrough for babies who would previously have needed life-saving blood transfusions. Light therapy is now used in all maternity hospitals. Before this, prenatal jaundice was the leading cause of death in small babies.

Colour in our daily life

We even describe ourselves in terms of colour. We say someone has a 'grey personality' or we 'see her true colours'. We're feeling, 'in the pink', or 'have the 'blues'. A person has had a 'colourful life' and when angry 'sees red'. They may be 'green with envy' or 'yellow with cowardice'. It seems we attach great importance to our relationship with colour. I know that when someone is described as colourless I imagine a dull, lifeless type, devoid of all joy. A person without the vibrancy and animation — well, the colour, in life.

'It seems that colour isn't just a shade of light, but an attribute of life itself.'

Colour is intricately involved in our lives far more than we realize. Every morning when choosing a shirt, tie, skirt or a T-shirt, we are making subconscious decisions about which colours we wear, therefore either which frequency of light we feel we need today, or which colour we want to radiate out to the world. Personally, in that brief moment of choosing the day's skirt, dress or shirt, I'm setting the tone for the day.

For instance, I go through orange phases: this is a second, pelvic chakra (see Chapter Four) colour, which reflects or draws me to creativity and sensuality. Vibrant blues are good for communication (fifth, throat chakra) days. Perhaps it's the morning of an important meeting, or I feel I need help today in communicating with my patients.

'Or I might just sense that I have weak throat energy,
and the beginnings of an infection.
In this case perhaps I'll choose to wear my lapis lazuli necklace.'

Of course jewellery is another way of using colour. For millennia women have been attracted to the pure hues of various crystals and stones, especially diamonds, the facets of which reflect all colours.

"The real voyage of discovery consists not in seeking new lands but in having new eyes."
—**Marcel Proust**

Women make these decisions instantly and subconsciously, as do men with their shirts and ties. But why not make them consciously? The more we pay attention to this, the more we can make colours work for us.

Greens and pinks support the heart, related to love. Most likely wearing these colours would reflect my inner need for love, or more self-love. Alternatively, perhaps this is the energy I wish to radiate out into the world, to share my heart's love.

Our business dress is very representative of the energies we wish to invoke. For example, a red suit or tie is a strong indicator of assertiveness and power. It's impossible to imagine a pushover or indecisive type wearing this colour!

On the other hand, how many business women would wear a lilac or purple suit? This colour, so beloved by the Roman nobility, is very spiritual, being associated with the sixth and seventh chakras, in the head. It just doesn't seem to fit into the male dominated, combative business world.

Black, a combination of primary colours, absorbs all colour frequencies, reflecting none. It's been said that people who favour black tend to feel the need to absorb all the light they can — I believe it!

*'It's been estimated that of the five senses,
most of our information about the outside world comes to us
through our eyes, in visual form, which is seen as patterns of colour.
Therefore small changes in the frequency of these colours could be
predicted to have an enormous effect on our minds and bodies.'*

Vision and the brain

We think we see light with our eyes, but in fact the eyes are adept at changing what we see (light) into electric messages the brain can then understand. On looking at an object, the lens of the eye focuses and it then inverts the image, which is seen on the retina, at the back of the eyeball. After this there's a chemical reaction, leading to a nerve impulse.

'This is a typical example of our body's ability to change light energy into other forms — light to chemical to electrical.'

The nerve impulse then travels up the optical nerve to the brain's visual cortex, where the electrical impulses are translated into meaningful patterns. These patterns are what our visual image becomes. These patterns, which of course are only our perceptions of an image, are like any other automatic response, and are of course open to the influences of past experience — seeing is in the eye of the beholder.

"The light of the body is the eye: if therefore thine eye be single, thy whole body shall be full of light."
—**Matthew 6:22,**

This explains why 10 different people who witness the same accident will later give a totally different version!

'Biologically, seeing is done by the mind, not the eyes.'

Sight is not automatic, but rather a learned, practised ability. For example, someone who's been blind since birth, and then had their sight restored, will at first just see light, not meaningful images. Then they learn the 'meaning' of those light patterns, as their brain becomes adept at processing this new sensory information. To complicate matters, what we see isn't really the object itself, but its reflected light.

'We don't perceive matter at all, but light.'

Vision is more than seeing...

When light enters the eye, not all the light is involved in imaging. Some light goes directly from the eye's retina at the back of the eyeball to the hypothalamus gland. The hypothalamus is known as the 'master control gland' of the body, as it controls the pituitary functions.

'It is difficult to think of anything in the body that the pituitary gland doesn't do, from controlling fertility, reproductive cycles and sexual development, growth hormones in developing cells and bones, to the thyroid and our metabolic rate, adrenal output and therefore stress responses and blood sugar control, as well as the vital kidney function!'

Seeing the light: the pineal gland

From the hypothalamus, light is then further sent on to the pineal gland, a tiny cone-shaped organ right in the centre of the brain that was only recently discovered by modern medicine.

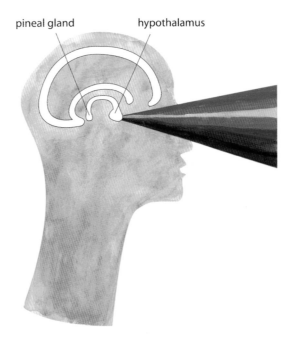

However, much is written about it in ancient Egyptian and Greek literature. Descartes, the French philosopher, described it as the 'seat of the soul', and it's interesting to compare this with the eyes, thought of as 'windows of the soul'.

The pineal is what's commonly known as the 'third eye', not an inaccurate description considering that the gland closely resembles the structure of the eye and has cells which react directly to light.

Also, both the eye and pineal are derived from similar evolutionary origins. In some primitive spineless animals, the pineal actually takes the place of eyes, and is situated near the front of their brains, where it reacts to light. In sub-mammals such as fish, frogs and birds, the pineal can actually detect light.

In birds it is thought that the pineal contains magnetic material which is used to navigate. The gland is magneto-electric, capable of monitoring magnetic fields round the Earth and helping the bird's body align in space.

'The pineal controls the circadian rhythm, essential especially in animals, as it regulates appropriate seasonal changes such as when to start growing a thick woolly coat.'

A mammal can't wait till the snow comes, as it will be too late to grow a protective coat by then. Something internal has to indicate to the body a seasonal appropriateness, especially with hibernating and breeding habits, as the timing will be vital for the animals' welfare — for example young must be born when both weather conditions and food availability will support them.

In humans the pineal produces melatonin, a hormone known to regulate sleep/wake cycles, produced as we sleep, and responsible for our circadian rhythm. At the maximum level when we are children, the amount of melatonin produced diminishes with age. It has developed a popular reputation as a hormone of anti-aging, or rejuvenation.

Melatonin itself is a photoreceptor — sensitive to light — produced by some animals in the retina of the eye (again, mainly at night). It's also an antioxidant that is capable of preventing age-related macular degeneration, the most common cause of blindness in the elderly.[2]

At this stage not a lot is known about the pineal gland. However, the recent discovery of a pineal tract of nerves going from the hypothalamus gland to the pineal, then a feedback nerve loop in the reverse, suggests how important this gland could be. This anatomical connection indicates that both these two vital glands are communicating and influencing one another.

'If the pineal gland has influence over the hypothalamus gland, which as previously stated controls the pituitary, then it has an effect on almost everything in the body, from growth, to fertility, to stress.'

Mal-illumination

We now know how important natural sunlight is for bone development, as the body needs the effect of sun on skin to produce vitamin D. Ricketts, a bone disease that had become increasingly rare because of improving nutritional standards, has been noted to be on the increase in cases of Middle Eastern women, especially those living in a much less sunny climate than would be normal for them. As they wear clothes that cover up most of their skin, they're just not getting strong enough sunlight to balance their hormone systems, therefore they are not forming strong enough bones.

This may be the tip of the iceberg, however. Mal-illumination is a term coined by scientist Dr John Ott[3] who extensively studied the effects of artificial lighting both in medical schools and research hospitals. Of course, modern man spends much of his day under fluorescent lighting, which does not have the full EM spectrum of natural light, generally containing only around three of the seven EM spectral colours.

'Dr Ott suggested that mal-illumination was a state akin to malnutrition, where our body would display adverse health changes because it wasn't receiving the sustenance it needed for perfect health.'

Early studies focused on the lifespan of mice, keeping them in different types of light. It was found that in fluorescent light they lived an average of 8.2 months, and those in natural light managed to extend their lives to 16.1 months. His classroom studies on schoolchildren found that when comparing natural full-spectrum lighting with unnatural lighting, there was a marked improvement in learning abilities, attention, hyperactivity and irritability in the natural light.

Colour in healing

Considering all the functions of the hypothalamus, pituitary and pineal glands, it doesn't take much of a quantum leap (small light joke) to imagine colours affecting our health and moods.

Healing with colour has quite a historical provenance…

The ancient Egyptians, a civilized society capable of fantastically complex engineering feats, built intricate light-healing temples. These would be arranged so that a sick person could be positioned under an inlet of sunlight. The light would then be filtered by precious and semi-precious gemstones to alter its frequency and therefore properties.

Heliopolis (city of the sun) in the ancient world was a centre of healing using sunlight.

Hippocrates, called the 'father of modern medicine', believed in the medical use of light, and used it for a number of ailments.

Some colour therapists prescribe some patients different coloured water to drink as appropriate. This art is rather like any natural therapy in that it addresses the emotional as well as physical state of the patient.

Medically, light is used in the same way as a laser for many skin conditions (acne, rosacea, psoriasis), healing of bony fractures and also in types of cancers, and neonatal jaundice.

As Jacob Lieberman pointed out in his excellent book *Light Medicine of the Future"*

"If parts of the EM spectrum are harmful to our health,
such as x-rays, nuclear radiation and so on,
then it is reasonable to think that the parts of which we're aware
and which surround us — colours — might be healing."

Colour in food

Plants derive their energy from the Sun, and sunlight is a full-spectrum light. This means that it contains all the shades of colour. We're beginning to realize more and more that the colours of fruit and vegetables correspond to their health-giving properties. For instance the red colour found in apple skins is due to the compound anthocyanin, which is responsible for the red and blue of blueberries, cranberries and other red/blue flowers and fruit. This compound is also an antioxidant, with health-giving properties. Apple growers know that this attractive red colour, so important to their sales, is dependent on light as the apples won't become red if grown in the shade.

'Scientists have now pinpointed the gene responsible for the apple's health-giving anthocyanin production, and found that it's activated by light.' [4]

Lycopene is the natural red pigment responsible for the colour of tomatoes. It is a cancer-fighting antioxidant, shown to be protective against cancers of the prostate, lung and colon. When tomatoes are picked unripe in order to soften during shipment, it's been found that even though the tomatoes appear red and ripe, because of lack of sunlight, they don't have the same amounts of this health-giving substance lycopene.

There has been a lot of research on the relationship between cancer and lycopene levels. Perhaps more interesting research (for gourmets!) has shown how heating tomatoes helps to release lycopene and how olive oil, if added, helps the body's lycopene absorption.[5,6]

'Nobel laureate Albert Szent-Gyorgi[7] noted that light itself could be considered a nutrient.'

All our nutrition ultimately comes from plants, whose energy comes from the Sun. In addition, Szent-Gyorgi's research found that many of the body's enzyme systems and hormones — chemicals that make everything work — were sensitive to different colours. Other researchers[8] found that the use of certain colours could increase the activity of enzymes by 500%. Again, we're finding that not only is light vital for the correct functioning of our bodies, but the actual light colour — its frequency — is also important.

'If physicists agree that matter is frozen light, then our food with its many shades is surely materialized colour.'

There are a number of exercises throughout this book, and it's essential to be in the correct calm physiological state to gain maximum benefit. The most important thing in achieving this is the way you breathe.

Breathing in the light

The breath, or our ability to breathe, is basically the difference between a live and dead body.

'The breath is life. How we breathe is directly related to how we live.
We breathe as much as we want to live.'

It helps, doing all these exercises, to remind yourself that you're breathing in the light of life, and to remind yourself at each breath how important it is. Our lungs are pear-shaped, with the bulk of our lung volume housed inside the lower ribs.

'Due to our everyday rushed and stressful lives,
we tend to be in the habit of only using the top third — the upper chest.
This means that there's a whole lot of stale air down there not getting
oxygenated. Do you ever feel stale?'

All the exercises in this book should be accompanied by this natural, relaxed breath. I do the following exercise with many anxious and stressed patients, with immediate success.

Mark, a brilliant 37-year-old architect, was successful and professionally fulfilled, however he had no time for his family and worried constantly about meeting deadlines and client pressures. Typically, he couldn't even describe why he felt bad, and just kept saying that he was tired all the time and 'felt dreadful'. A quick glance told me that most of his discomfort was directly due to bad breathing technique, as what he was doing was exactly the opposite to the way his lungs were meant to work. What he didn't realize was that the natural pattern of expansion and contraction of the ribcage was vital for wellbeing.

*'The exercise below was very gratifying to teach as, within 10 minutes,
Mark, who'd felt simply horrible because of stress, felt 90% better!'*

As I explained, there are many physiological reasons why he felt so bad because of the unnatural breathing pattern. When any of us feel anxious or worried about something, the ancient physiological response of 'run from saber-toothed tiger' mechanism kicks in. Stress hormones adrenalin and cortisol cause a shallowness and increase in breathing rate, raising pulse and blood pressure. Muscle fibres are shortened and bunched, all ready for a quick sprint of escape, but this wasn't helping Mark in his meetings with demanding clients.

*'In Mark's situation all it led to was back and neck muscle tension,
as well as chest muscle contraction causing chest pains,
which convinced him he was going to have a heart attack.'*

In the fight-or-flight stress response, the breathing becomes more rapid and superficial in order to get more oxygen in the short term to those 'ready to sprint' muscles. This then alters the electrolyte balance of the body (sodium, potassium and so on) leading to tingling and numbness of hands as well as more muscular tension. Also, the hyperventilation causes a decrease in the lung gas carbon dioxide, a gas that is known to have a calming effect on the brainstem and brain. Talk about a vicious cycle.

'Like most men, Mark was happy to comply with my advice on daily exercise, however wouldn't have fitted in some lengthy breathing programme.'

Of course, aerobic exercise (anything getting one out of breath) is the natural antidote to the fight-or-flight response, as muscles will be stretched and relaxed, blood circulated briskly, flushing out waste products of excess stress hormones.

The solution: I taught Mark how to practise this technique on a regular basis. It's simple, and we managed to fit just three minutes three times daily into his hectic schedule.

Use this breathing technique throughout all the exercises in this book. This is the breath of light, and life, so make the intent that each breath is health giving, rejuvenating, and filling you with joy.

Exercise 1: Breathing in the Light

Instructions

Sit upright, in a quiet place, at a time when you feel you have five minutes to yourself. It will help to close the eyes.

Firstly, focus on the feeling of air going in and out of the nostrils. Imagine you're breathing in light itself. Placing one hand on your abdomen, feel it rise and fall as you breathe.

On the out-breath, as air is expelled, your hand should be drawn in, nearer the spine. Sometimes this all seems a bit hard, so in the beginning just focus on the out-breath, and pulling your stomach in, then simply relax on the in-breath, and your stomach area will naturally inflate.

Like a balloon filling with air, your lower lungs (and therefore your abdomen) should expand on the in-breath, so your hand should move away from your spine.

Exercise 2: Rebalancing Energy with Colour

This is a simple, amazingly powerful exercise to rebalance the body's energies at the level of its colour frequencies. By bringing all the colours of the EM spectrum into the body, you'll receive the energy required for balance or healing, on all levels — physical, emotional, mental and spiritual.

To avoid intellectualizing the process and using your mind to work out which colours you might need, I advise using the whole colour spectrum. Each colour must be imagined to be true and clear, like a jewel.

Instructions

Sit comfortably in a peaceful place where you won't be disturbed. It's always best to have an upright spine, so try not to slump.

Practise the breathing technique of Exercise 1, with eyes closed.

Starting at the beginning of the spectrum, imagine the colour red being beamed down through the crown of your head, absorbed throughout your body. Every cell and strand of DNA is vibrating as it is bathed in red, absorbing its EM frequency.

After 20 to 30 seconds, do the same with orange. Take three to five breaths with each colour. Move through orange, yellow, green, blue, indigo and violet.

Because of the nature of our physiology, the breath will carry the EM frequency vibration of specific colours through our lungs, filtering through to the blood and then into every cell and DNA strand. In this way we can truly integrate these frequencies.

"All living things, including the Earth, radiate electromagnetic energy."

Chapter 4

Connecting to the Body's Light Systems — Indian Chakras

Just as the physical body has many functional systems, such as nervous, endocrine, skeletal, so does the energy body. The best known energy systems are the Indian chakra and the Chinese meridian system.'

THE CHAKRA AND MERIDIAN energy systems have been known for thousands of years, most certainly predating our recent knowledge of our bodies releasing electromagnetic energy. In discussing these internal systems, you will see many references to light.

We will refer to the visible light spectrum, red through violet. Or we might imagine light as laser beams (laser is a stream of light) connecting us in different ways.

Throughout this book there are exercises based on using the hands' EM energy, so first we need to explore the light energy of the hands.

Hands of light

Western medicine has made a quantum leap in reversing the death rate in childbirth and pregnancy, and everyone's now living to a grand old age, so let's be thankful for it.

'However, perhaps because of the increasing drug and technology reliance of this type of medicine, people are turning to ancient techniques to "fill in the gaps".'

I rarely meet anyone nowadays who hasn't been doing Reiki, the Tibetan healing art brought to the world by a Japanese doctor. Using sacred symbols, the usual method is by positioning hands in specific positions on the body.

'Laying on of hands', in the Christian tradition, Prannic healing from India, as well as versions from Polynesia, New Zealand and China, all use different mystical traditions and have vastly different cultural heritages, the commonality being in the use of hands touching or near the body. Previously this type of healing was thought to be either largely 'in the mind', placebo effect or just a comfort factor success story. However,

scientists are now finding out more and more about the power of our hands, apparently little hot spots of electromagnetic activity.

'Our palms radiate infrared, ultraviolet, infrasonic, microwave, electric, magnetic and scalar energies.'

American researchers Drs. Becker and Zimmerman, using a highly sensitive magnetic 'Superconducting Quantum Interference Device', measured the Qigong practitioner's 'healing' hands energy. They found that the electromagnetic field coming from the healer's hands during a healing was at least 1000 times that of normal.

Interestingly, studies done on these Chinese Qigong healers found that whilst the energy from the palms surges as expected during a healing, there was no rise in the healer's body EM or current flow, as would be expected if this extra energy were coming from their body's cells.

'The only possible scientific conclusion to be drawn was that this extra energy was coming from another energy source, such as the Earth itself.'

We all know intuitively that the touch of our hands is therapeutic. In all cultures touch is a central part of social interaction, whether shaking hands, as a hug, or patting the arm of a friend in distress. Without being aware of it, we all use this healing power.

Of course, a Chinese Qigong master has perfected and optimized this light radiation; however, even the average person has these basic emissions, and is therefore capable of consciously using them. A little bit like playing the piano, anyone can do it, but some will have more natural talent than others.

As these chapters progress, we'll discuss using our hands' electromagnetic light radiation to connect with and to nurture the other light centres of the body.

'In this way we can work with our own body's energy,
to optimize the flow and the strength of light, to heal ourselves and others.'

What are chakras?

Chakras are good examples of light in our bodies. The word *chakra* means 'wheel of light', reflecting their moving and spinning quality.

According to ancient wisdom, chakras are very important bodily energy centres in the visible (red through violet) light spectrum. They extend up our body, in a vertical line. There are seven major ones, located at the tailbone, belly, solar plexus, heart, throat, third eye and crown of the head.

Linked with the system of yoga, they were first written about in the Indian Vedas – manuscripts dating from the second millennium BC.

'According to the Sufis, the nature of the Universe is to spin…'

Our Universe is composed of spinning wheels of energy. The Earth rotates on its own axis and also round the Sun, forming our solar system. Our solar system also rotates, as does our galaxy, in a giant spiral.

In ancient Greece, the 'Greek Key' is a spiral pattern found everywhere in Mycenaean and Cycladic artefacts, on carvings, belts, jewellery and armour.

Going smaller, the electron has its own spin axis round the nucleus of a cell, and our DNA are spiral. In fact photons, the smallest unit of light, are themselves released in the form of a spiral. We could think of the wheel as a circle of life, moving through all aspects of existence.

I like to think of chakras as increased areas of energy and sensitivity in the body, which connect our physical being to the non-physical realms.

'Chakras are the bridge between matter and consciousness.'

We all live with electricity and roughly understand the concept of the electrical energy (electron) flow, so I'm going to use this analogy.

'Chakras can be thought of as transducers of light.'

Remember that light is both emitted and received by us. In the same way that a loudspeaker converts electrical into sound energy, chakras will convert information from the sea of energy in which we live into data that we can then understand and process. Things we don't take in with our conscious mind will still be sensed by this system, so we receive energetic feedback from what's happening around us, whether this is in nature or at a party.

Have you ever had the experience of walking into a room where people are arguing and feeling that you could 'cut the energy with a knife'? Or felt the serenity and peace at the top of a mountain, or a special place in nature?

'So, chakras sense energy around us and translate that vibration into a form that can be understood by us.'

For example: you go home late, walk in the house to see your wife standing in the kitchen with her back to you. She hasn't said a word and you can't see her face, however you know she's mad. You can feel the heat rising from her, anger radiating out. How? Your body simply feels it. Using past experience as a guide, the brain then works out the meaning of this energy — anger.

We pick up all sorts of energetic cues the moment we meet someone: for instance, instantly we might distrust a stranger. Or, just 'know' that someone is reliable and kind.

To continue the electrical example, it could also be said that chakras are also transformers of energy. Meaning that in transferring energy from one system to another (think of an A/C current circuit stepping down voltage), the energy is subtly changed so that it won't blow our systems.

Chakra connection to illnesses

Chakras are correlated to the type of bodily energy where they are situated. This may be on an emotional, mental or physical level. This means that we can directly work with the body's energies (therefore health) by strengthening and clearing the chakras.

'As well as being sensitive to energies around us,
chakras are also reactive to our own emotions.
Negative ones such as guilt, grief or anger being the most damaging.'

When I first worked as a busy Hong Kong family doctor, I developed asthma, which would manifest itself, three times yearly, in the form of a wheezy bronchitis. I would be exhausted for a month before this would clear, no matter which medication I took. Having seen the best chest specialists and been diagnosed as an asthmatic, I was on the usual inhalers; however, things were worsening.

At that time I was also working as an on-air doctor for a radio station. One day at the station I bumped into an energy healer called Victoria Bullis. She was great fun, and though up until then I had no time for anything 'alternative', I liked her so decided to let her help me. Over the next month she worked on my energies and, miraculously, I got better.

She also encouraged me to work on my own heart energies, or fourth chakra. She explained how wearing this chakra's colour — green — would support it, and even eating green food would increase its energy. This all seemed a little far-fetched; however, thinking it would do no harm, and being sick of my dependency on medication, I gave it a go. I did all of this very secretly, of course!

'She explained how asthma and other chest problems are considered a disorder of the fourth, heart chakra, and related to affairs of the heart, such as sadness or grief.'

In my case, my asthma was not related to grief over death, but sadness over things in my life I considered a failure (relationships, and so on). I tried all of this, along with talking to Victoria, and much to my surprise, was able to come off all asthma medications over the next four months.

Another common example of illness in relation to the chakras is digestive problems, which are so common in Western society.

'In this way of thinking, the third chakra is affected by negative emotions and is often associated with indigestion, acidity and ulcers. Think of folklore and "worrying yourself sick".'

Apparently, around 20% of the population has irritable bowel syndrome, leading to abdominal bloating, gas, and either diarrhoea or constipation. Of course partly this could be due to poor eating habits, or not eating enough fibre. However, in chakra terminology, we'd explain that although this is true and undoubtedly a major cause, endemic in society is a constant worry about other people's opinions of oneself. This is a basic form of low self-esteem, which is a function of the third chakra. It relates to 'sense of self', and is situated over the stomach in the upper abdomen.

'Our physical organs are susceptible to toxins, such as viruses or chemicals. In the same way, the chakras are affected by emotional toxins, such as anger and guilt, or not feeling good enough.'

Chakra Properties and Clinical Examples

This is not meant to be a comprehensive list. For further reading I recommend having a look at the fantastic ground-breaking work by medical intuitive Caroline Myss. Her books *Anatomy of The Spirit,* and *Why People Don't Heal and How They Can* are truly illuminating.

As well as the colours associated with each chakra, I've noted the sound and musical note.

'In addition to using colour, there is another method of balancing the chakras — chanting, singing or just saying the sound will send out a vibration that will then both cleanse and harmonize with the energy of each chakra.'

First chakra

I like to start at the first, or base chakra, situated at the bottom of your spine. This is the grounding, red-coloured chakra — our connection to the energies of the Earth. Being the base chakra, it represents our survival on Earth, whether financial or any other form of security.

It seems that even the most wealthy people can go through life feeling financially insecure, worrying constantly and penny pinching. They fear losing their money, and have no faith in their ability to sustain themselves in life.

Other challenges for this chakra would be life events that threaten our basic security, such as losing a job, getting divorced, death of a parent, and so on.

A good way to connect with your chakra energy is to dance with the energies of each chakra. Dancing with the first chakra would be very primeval: to an African drum beat with feet firmly planted on the ground, barefoot, connecting to the Earth's vibrations.

This is because the Earth is the basic source of all that sustains us on the physical plane.

'Disorders associated with this chakra tend to reflect our issues of insecurity in surviving in this world, and fears, especially financial. Remember the old wives' tale of low back pain being related to worries over money?'

A list of potential ailments associated with weak first chakra energy system:

Disease
- Low back pain, long standing
- Haemorrhoids, rectal tumours
- Depression
- Disease of bones and bone marrow

Emotional
- fear of poverty, providing necessities
- fear of law, or punishment
- never feeling part of a community

Also associated with the first chakra:

Colour	*Sound*	*Note*
• Red	• Lam	• C

Second chakra

Mid-belly, halfway between pubic and umbilicus, this orange chakra reflects our creativity and sexuality. What could be more creative than producing a new life? If dancing with this chakra's energy we want to move our hips and to belly-dance, or salsa.

This chakra is important in manifesting, meaning creating what we want in this life. Also, it's involved in all our relationships, not just romantic. As you can imagine, this is one HUGE area.

A list of potential ailments associated with weak second chakra energy system:

Disease
- Gynaecological, urinary problems
- Low back pain
- Sexual dysfunctions and potency
- Pelvic and prostate problems

Emotional
- Sexual guilt
- Issues around money
- Control, relationship issues
- Blocked creativity

Also associated with the second chakra:

Colour	Sound	Note
• Orange	• Vam	• D

Fiona, an attractive, petite 35-year-old banker, had disabling menstrual pains and had recently developed two ovarian cysts. Also, every time she met a new boyfriend she'd get an attack of vaginal yeast. Previously as healthy as a horse, she was very upset and depressed about all this, feeling it was ruining her otherwise well-controlled life.

Most patients want a physical explanation and immediate cure for their symptoms; however, Fiona had a lot of insight and was willing to discuss any emotional and relationship issues. One day, she announced, 'This all started after my husband left me three years ago. I wonder why?'

Further discussion revealed that he'd cheated on her and lied. It became obvious that not only did she not trust men, she no longer even trusted in her own choices of men. The moment she met a new man to whom she was attracted, all her fears regarding betrayal and rejection would surface.

This was not a conscious process that she was aware of, but rather it would surface through physical symptoms relating to the second chakra.

Because she kept herself so busy as a banker with a 10-hour work day, these fears didn't percolate through to her conscious mind, where she could have seen them clearly. Instead, they would bubble away in her subconscious, manifesting as second chakra physical symptoms. For Fiona, psychology was the best choice in unravelling these subconscious patterns. As she did this, the physical symptoms slowly diminished.

Six months later, this attractive lady bounced into my office with a big smile and a ring on her finger. She'd been able to trust again, and was planning her wedding.

Third chakra

Located at our solar plexus, below the bottom of the breast bone, this is a bright yellow 'Sun'. It's our sense of self — our personal power.

This is about self-confidence, listening to our own intuition, doing what we know to be right rather than being swayed by others who supposedly know better. It's all about not giving away our power. Disorders may reflect as:

Disease
- Liver, pancreas problems
- Stomach, indigestion, ulcer problems
- Intestinal problems

Emotional
- Self-esteem and respect
- Trust, fear
- Burdened by responsibility

Also associated with the third chakra:

Colour	*Sound*	*Note*
• Yellow	• Ram	• E

I had a patient called Jane, a grey-haired 50-year-old office manager who worked incredibly hard and worried all the time about her performance. She suffered from 'chronic dyspepsia', an overproduction of stomach acidity causing upper abdominal discomfort and bloating. Painfully thin, she seemed worn down by life. In constant anxiety, her shoulders and back muscles were so tight and she was always in pain.

Spending time explaining the workings of the body, I firstly suggested she relax the physical body's muscle tension through massage. After all, it would be impossible to relax mentally in such a tight, stressed body. We dealt with the toxic anxiety by teaching her breathing and meditation exercises, which calm the mind.

*'Little by little, over the next two months we noticed that
Jane's abdominal symptoms were going,
and were now 100% treated by her daily medication.'*

She was having more fun in life, making time for her friends and swimming regularly. At her prompting I reduced, then stopped, all her anti-acidity medications.

Jane remained well, now having more fun in life and seeing her friends regularly. The exercise and meditation were continued on a regular basis, as she now made time for her own body to heal, and to get her life back under control. She's learnt to empower herself, taking charge in a way she couldn't before.

Somehow, even without psychotherapy, Jane had managed to let go of her third chakra worry and guilt issues.

'It seems that if these toxic emotions are not processed
(dealt with rather than being ignored or suppressed),
they're stored in the chakras, leading to energy flow blockages
and, therefore, malfunction of the organs
with which the chakras are associated.'

Fourth chakra

Over the heart, this is love. Not just romantic love, but love for nature, and our connectedness with all things. In this we mustn't forget love for ourselves, and also for humanity in general. This chakra is a beautiful emerald green colour; however, some see the higher attributes of love — unconditional love for all things — as a vibrant pink. Either (or both) is okay.

Disease

- Heart problems
- Asthma
- Chest infections, lung cancer
- Upper back, shoulder pains

Emotional

- Issues with commitment or selfishness
- Issues with love or anger
- Issues with grief, trust or forgiveness

Also associated with the fourth chakra:

Colour	*Sound*	*Note*
• Green/pink	• Yam	• F

Fifth chakra

The throat chakra radiates a sky-blue colour and is related to communication. This is about speaking truth and expressing ourselves. Being assertive and not saying 'yes' when we mean 'no'.

More than speaking our truth, it's about daring to live it. In expressing who we really are, rather than an artificial image that conforms to others' expectations, we step into our truth/power.

Disease
- Throat, mouth ulcer, gum problems
- Thyroid dysfunction and jaw problems

Emotional
- Use of free will and power of assertion
- Issues with judgment (others or oneself) and criticism
- Speaking your truth and making decisions

Also associated with the fifth chakra:

Colour	*Sound*	*Note*
• Blue	• Hum	• G

Janice was a 41-year-old experienced English teacher from New Zealand. For the past six months she'd had bout after bout of serious hoarseness and throat infections, requiring weeks off work.

'It's because my job involves talking all day long', she whispered painfully. I didn't want to antagonize her by pointing out that all teachers talk a lot as part of their job, and that she's been doing just that for many healthy years.

Instead, I gently asked if she's been having any communication problems lately. Perhaps at work, not managing to get on with her boss? At home, is she able to say what she wants to her husband, and is he hearing it? It didn't take long for her to get this point.

'Yes, I'm having real problems at work getting my point of view across with my boss. I'm getting more and more frustrated at not being listened to, and was thinking of resigning.'

I explained that these communication problems would 'weaken the energy' and 'reduce the immunity' around the throat area, leading to her problems. We agreed that she would work on new and better ways to get her point across. She hadn't been aware of a connection between these different areas of her life, and was happy to give this a go, rather than taking round after round of antibiotics. Even though an instant cure was not on the horizon, it helped to get insight into why illness had suddenly emerged out of nowhere.

For most people, understanding the cause of illness makes all the difference as they can then feel empowered to change.

Sixth chakra

The indigo third eye is either mid-forehead or between the eyebrows. Its function lies in seeing both inner and outer worlds in a number of ways.

This is the power of our foresight and intuition. Anyone with psychic 'seeing' abilities or blessed with a 'knowingness' about how future events will unfold has a well-developed third eye.

It's associated with our physical vision as we interpret light waves reflected off our surroundings in order to make a map of the environment. It is also the vision in our dreams that helps us form our intuition, as we see our way through different situations. This inner vision is what will then manifest our reality.

Disease
- The head and nervous system, sinus
- Blindness and deafness
- Epilepsy and learning problems

Emotional
- Poor self image and feelings of inadequacy
- Being closed to others' ideas, or over-thinking
- Not learning from past experience

Also associated with the sixth chakra:

Colour	Sound	Note
• Indigo	• Om	• A

Michael, a successful lawyer, suffered repeated sinus infections. Miserable and painful, they'd last two to three weeks, during which time he'd be tired and unable to concentrate or think at his normal level. Monthly flying on business just added to the problem, as the sinuses can't function in the low-humidity cabin environment.

A classic third eye problem, the root of this energy blockage lay in two areas. Firstly, in the intensely competitive and aggressive business environment, there was a constant struggle of one-upmanship, leading to his emotions swinging between inferiority and superiority.

Also, by the nature of Michael's work he lived 100% in his mind, over-thinking and over-processing every small detail of both his legal work and home life.

'Like most successful people, he was extremely intuitive;
however, this ability was becoming clouded by conflicting thoughts.
Instead of allowing free flow of his psychic powers,
his third eye was jammed with thought.'

In his case, what helped a lot was to find relaxation that involved the right side of his brain. The left side was so over-used by rationalizing, to bring balance he needed to find a creative, artistic hobby.

This was more easily achieved than I had thought; he was already highly intuitive and knew he was stuck in a rut in his going to the gym and occasional golf lifestyle. There were two things he'd always wanted to do but never had time for. One was learning the piano, the other going for painting lessons. He went away determined to make time for at least one of these creative activities.

'Either would be the perfect vehicle to unblock the stagnant energies
that allowed his immune system to malfunction.'

Seventh chakra

At the crown of the head, this colour is either violet or white, as white is a composite of all the other colours. This is our connection to divinity, or some may say to our soul, or higher self.

This is where we can access higher wisdom — not from an earthly outlook but an overview from high up — a broader perspective. The dance invoking these upper chakras tends to be directed upwards, as though petitioning God. On tiptoe, or with arms stretched up.

Disease
- Whole of the muscular and skeletal systems
- Depression and chronic fatigue
- Extreme sensitivities, like skin problems

Emotional
- Lack of faith and trust in life
- Lack of interest or courage

Also associated with the seventh chakra:

Colour	*Sound*	*Note*
• Violet	• Aum	• B
	(or the sound of silence)	

Exercise 3: Balancing the Chakras

Instructions

Starting with the first chakra, sitting upright, then repeat with all: Familiarize yourself with each chakra's colour, as above. Sit or lie with both hands on your body over the position of each chakra.

Remember, however, that although it's more comfortable to touch the front they also extend through to the back of the body so you will need to visualize the colour going right through.

Feeling the chakra, imagine the colour that's there right now. Give the chakra a score between one and 10, where one is the lowest vitality (or brightness) and 10 the highest. Do this quickly, based on feeling not thought. Give that chakra what it needs to be in balance by visualizing it to be a very pure, vibrant colour.

Move up to the next chakra. After working on all seven chakras, start again and see if there's a different score.

Remember, this is light healing, so be specific about the intensity of colour, seeing it as very true and representative of that part of the light spectrum. See red as an in-your-face, bright, post-box red, not pink or brown tones. Green is grass, bright green, not dark jade or pale mint.

*'In the second chakra example of indigestion (i.e. not digesting life)
as well as noting the third chakra to be a lower than average number,
you might note its colour.'*

It will most likely be a shade of yellow, however as you're not feeling well it could be anything from muddy yellow to pale lemon pastel. If so, imagine it to become a more brilliant colour, like a magnificent glowing sun, radiating health. People talk about cleansing as energizing chakras or spinning them in the correct direction. I wouldn't advise this. Setting the intent to balance them with colour is enough. Balance is a better concept than fixing, as our body knows exactly what to do.

Rainbow Light

The rainbow, naturally containing all colours of the spectrum, is perfect to use in our attempt to balance the chakras. This is easier for those who find it difficult to imagine colours, but who may find it easier to have a vision of a naturally occurring rainbow. Of course, you're the pot of gold at the end!

Instructions:

Sit upright, as before. Visualize a lovely rainbow arcing in the sky, in one of your favourite areas in nature. The end of the rainbow is flowing down over your head, as you stand or sit on the ground.

Visualize the rainbow moving through each chakra, starting with the seventh, at the top of your head. Move it down to the sixth at the forehead, then follow down through the rest.

At each chakra, all you need to do is feel that rainbow, and your body will absorb the colours it needs.

Chapter 5

Accessing the Body's Light Systems — Qi

Working with Qi

EXERCISES SUCH AS TAI Qi or Qigong, practised in China for thousands of years, are specifically designed to circulate Qi. In this book, I describe Qi as the energy flowing within the body, our life energy. However, it also has another meaning, in terms of more Universal energy.

Qi is the vital life force that ensures proper functioning of all the organs.

'Particular exercises shown here will stimulate
and energize specific organs, such as the lungs or intestine.'

Whether as part of a class or at home with a DVD, regular practice produces a feeling of well-being and mental clarity, as well as promoting balance in the functioning of the body's physiology.

Connecting to meridian light

According to this ancient way of viewing the body's energies, there are 12 main channels of energy flowing up and down our body, called meridians. The body's life-force energy, Qi, flows along these to bring vitality and health to all the tissues and organs.

*'Rather like an electrical current, it's important that
the correct amount of energy is flowing in the desired direction.
Too much, and there's a circuit overload or blowout.'*

Also, too little and there's not enough power, leading to malfunction.

At conception, an egg is fertilized, dividing into two, then four, then eight, continuing until the embryo is formed. It is thought that when it divides in two, the central division becomes our central meridian. This is the most important, primary meridian, running down the front of the body from lower lip to pubis. It forms a real barrier, or energetic protection for the body.

The other meridians run over the limbs, back and head, in certain directions. These are the channels along which lie the acupuncture points where needles could be inserted.

I love to connect to these meridians by using my palms to brush over my body, in the correct direction of each line. Doing this, the light energy of my hands will subtly stimulate the Qi in the meridians.

'It's something simple and free that we can all do to improve well-being, both physically and mentally. Again, we're consciously connecting the EM light in our hands to that of one of the body's energy systems — the meridians.'

Daily tune-up by circulating Qi

It took me ages to learn this routine exactly, but now it's completed in around a minute. Every time it is done, it stimulates the body's energies to flow smoothly and coherently — a personal tune-up.

'I have really benefitted from doing this in the middle of a busy day. It just seems to give me the clearing of stress required to stop an accumulation of the day's burdens on my system.'

The effect gets greater every time it's done, and it's rather like having the energy boosting effects of acupuncture daily. As a daily routine, preferably twice daily, this keeps the body in balance, and I find it also clears and calms the mind.

It is rare that a person won't feel subtly different after stimulating the paths of these meridians. Patients I've taught can feel the difference immediately, and I always give them written information to go home and practise.

It's important to use the palms. As discussed in Chapter 2 there are very good reasons hands-on healers have been using them for thousands of years. They really do radiate huge quantities of EM energy.

Exercise 4: Daily Tune-Ups Circulating Qi

Instructions

Starting with the governing meridian, brush both palms up your spine from the tailbone, up over the top of your head to the upper lip. Then do the central meridian, moving both hands down from lower lip to pubis. Completing this forms the 'Microcosmic Orbit', the essential Qi energetic band round the body.

Then do the rest of the meridians in the order shown in the drawings. At the end, finish again with the governing and central meridians. These two are the most important, forming a complete protective band round the body.

When moving over these meridians be sure to do both the left and right sides of the body. Each meridian is at its strongest in a certain two-hour period of the day.

Governing meridian

Place one hand at the bottom of the spine and move straight up your spine. Reach over your shoulder and try to touch the hand reaching up. If you can't do this, imagine it. Then with the top hand, trace the energy the rest of the way up your spine, over your head, over your nose, and to your top lip.

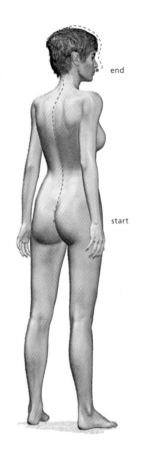

end

start

Central meridian

Place both hands on your lower lip and bring them straight down the front of your body to your pubis.

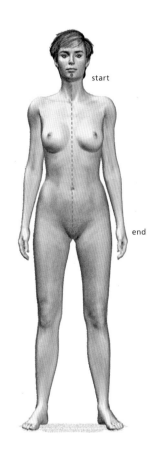

start

end

Stomach meridian
(7am to 9am)

Place both hands under the eyes, move down to your jawbone, then circle up the outside of your face to your forehead, and move down through your eyes to the collarbone. Move out at your collarbone, down over the chest, in at the waist, then out at the hips, straight down the front of the legs, and finish at the second toe.

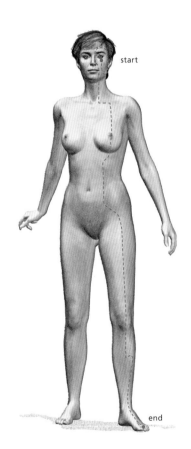

Spleen meridian
(9am to 11am)

Start at the outside corners of each big toe and go straight up the inside of your legs, moving out at your hips, up the side of your ribcage, and down to the lower outer ribcage.

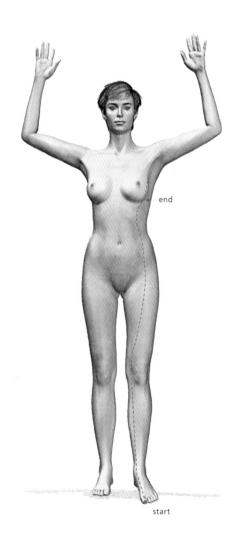

end

start

Heart meridian
(11am to 1pm)

Place your open hand underneath the opposite armpit on the same side as your little finger and trace straight down the inside of the arm and off the little finger.

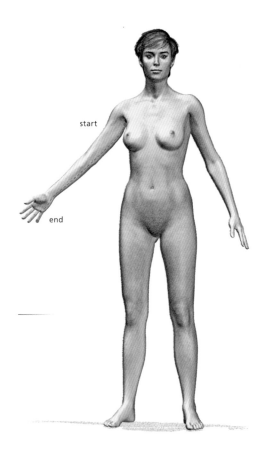

start

end

Small intestine
(1pm to 3pm)

Start at the back of the hand, going up from the small finger up the back of the arm. Go down at the back of the shoulder, then up to the cheekbone, and horizontally back to the ear.

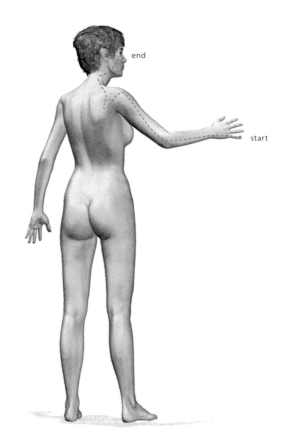

Bladder meridian (3pm to 5pm)

Firstly, with one hand, start on the forehead, move it up over the top of your head to connect with the other hand. Move both down the back then in and around your buttocks. Secondly, trace an outer line: starting at the upper back, go straight down to the back of the knees, in at the knees, down and finish at the small toes.

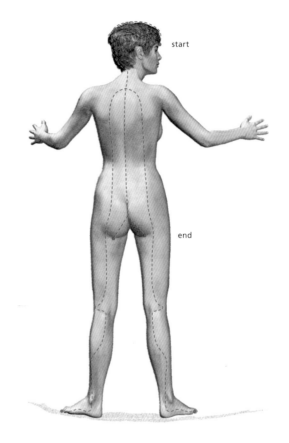

start

end

Kidney meridian
(5pm to 7pm)

Place your fingers under the ball of each foot, then circle round the inside of each ankle bone, going straight up the inside of the leg, groin, then the front of the body to K-27 acupuncture point. This is the small notch beneath the collar bone, on the inner side. K-27 is important, so take the opportunity to give it a good rub.

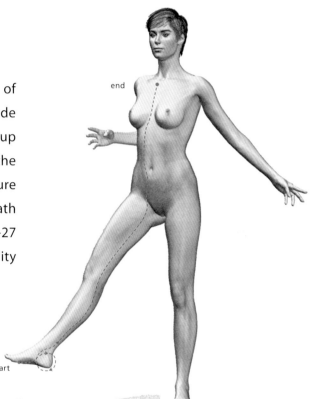

end

start

Pericardium meridian
(7pm to 9pm)

Place fingers of one hand at the outer side of the opposite breast, come up over the shoulder, then move up the inside of the arm, finishing at the middle finger.

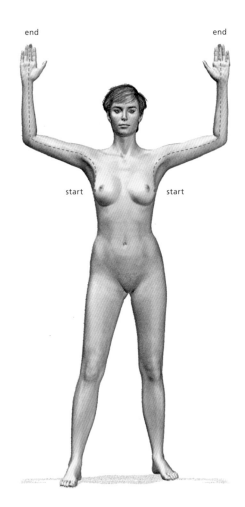

Triple warmer meridian
(9pm to 11pm)

On the back of your hand, starting at the ring finger, move straight up the outer arm to beneath your ear, curve round the back of the ear, ending at your temple.

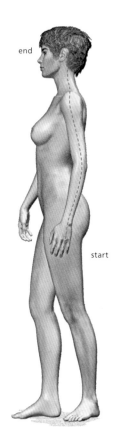

Gall bladder meridian
(11pm to 1am)

Placing the fingers of each hand on the outer eyebrows, move down to the ear opening, then straight up about two inches. Circle forward with your fingers, then loop back behind the ears. Go up over the crown of the head, moving down to the shoulders. Moving your arms behind you, go to the shoulder, moving down the side of the body as in the diagram. End at your fourth toe.

Start

end

Liver meridian
(1am to 3am)

Run the hands up from the big toes straight up the inside of the legs. Move out at the groin, up the ribcage, to finish in line with the nipples.

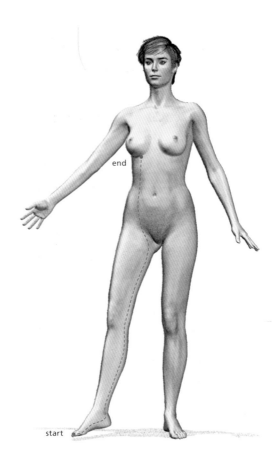

end

start

Lung meridian
(3am to 5am)

Place one hand under the opposite outer collar bone and circle it up over your shoulder, straight down your arm, and end at your thumb.

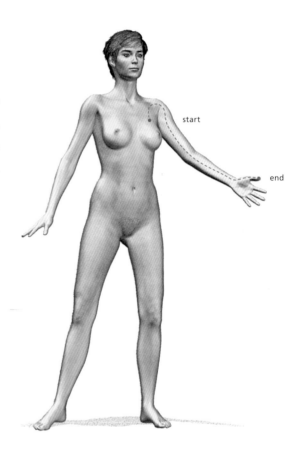

start

end

Large intestine
(5am to 7am)

Place the fingers of one hand at the end of the index finger of the opposite hand, go straight up the arm across the top of the shoulder, up the neck to the centre of the nostrils, then out to the outer corner of the opposite nostril. Finish in the same way as the start, with the Microcosmic orbit — governing and central meridian.

Continuous tune-up

The Qi energy, like DC current, must run in the correct direction in order to exert its influence. This fact has been noted in the original Chinese literature, as far back as the Huangdi Neijing two thousand years ago.

'It's amazing how quickly our meridians can become misdirected,
so that Qi no longer flows smoothly.
Any trauma will do this, however small.
Even having an upsetting thought will stagnate the meridian flow.
In the East, the concept of "balance" is very subtle!'

Therefore, do the above exercises as often during the day as you can manage, and watch as the benefits appear. There will be huge improvements in calmness, mental clarity and energy.

This is a great tune-up. However, if it is too much for you, try this simplified version.

Towel Drying

Using a towel to dry can be incorporated into a daily tune-up, if you move the towel in the correct direction. The basics are to remember to dry the arms down the insides, armpit to fingers, up the outsides. Dry the legs moving up the insides, inner ankle to groin, then down the outsides and down the front.

Of course, to benefit from the hands' energy, you don't need to restrict this to a post-shower experience. It's easy to regularly use the hands to brush light down the meridians in the same way.

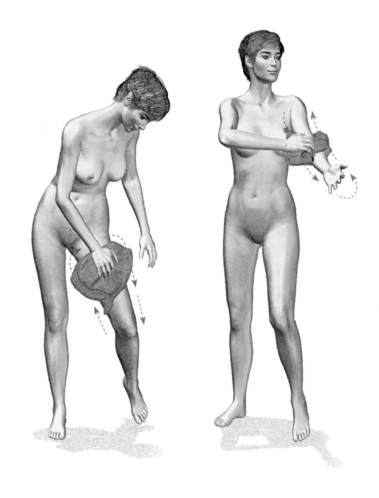

Improving health using meridians

Exercise 5: Intestinal problems

In any illness, knowledge of meridian energy flows can be used to promote healing. For example, with intestinal problems such as food poisoning or irritable bowel syndrome, try 'flushing' this meridian. This means clearing out any stagnating light energy, and encouraging the flow.

Instructions

Locate large intestine meridian. Connect to the meridian moving in the 'wrong' direction (i.e. nostril to finger) on both arms. Do three times in the correct direction (finger up to nostril).

Exercise 6: Lung problems

With lung problems such as bronchitis or asthma, use the same procedure in the lung meridian:

Instructions

Locate lung meridian. Connect to the meridians in the 'wrong' direction (thumb to chest) on both arms. Do three times in the correct direction.

Meridians for jet-lag and energy boosting

Exercise 7: For jet-lag

To adapt to a new time zone, focus on the meridian corresponding to the present time. This helps your body reset itself to the new time. (Note the times associated with meridians — when this energy is strongest.) In the new time zone, do these exercises as many times as you can during the day, using the appropriate meridians. If it's midday in your new time zone, it's heart time.

Instructions

As usual, connect to the central and governing meridians. Do all the meridians in normal order, except this time both start and finish with the heart meridian, in this way boosting heart, midday energy. Do central and governing meridians again.

Exercise 8: Energy boosting

Many people experience energy slumps in the afternoon. This is especially frustrating for housewives who are faced with an energetic child returning from school, talking nonstop and needing help with his homework! If it's 4pm, this is then bladder time.

Instructions:

As in the previous exercise, using your hands, connect to the central meridian to start. Do all meridians in normal order, except this time both start and finish with the bladder meridian, in this way boosting bladder, 4pm energy. Finish with the governing meridian.

Unblocking Qi

I met Sally, a rather cynical nurse from Texas, at a consciousness conference in Albuquerque. Sitting next to me in an energy workshop, she complained about being exhausted as the dry air at that altitude had brought on her asthma and sinusitis. Luckily for her the workshop revolved around stimulating the body's immune system by pressing on various key points, described below.

'After massaging these points on and off for a couple of hours,
much to her surprise Sally felt almost 100%.
The sinuses were unblocked, she had more energy
and her chest wasn't so tight.'

In the vast majority of people their light energy will be blocked in one or other point. You'll know if it's blocked if there is tenderness on pressure. Especially with patients who are generally tired, lacking energy and zest, I've found that there are two simple massage points that can make a huge difference to well-being: one is beneath the collar bone — this is one of the most important Chinese acupuncture points — K27. The other is on the ribcage beneath the nipple — L14.

'How often is it that you get in a panic not being able to find your keys while rushing to leave the house, only to notice that they're in your hand?'

This is an example of our brain not functioning in a stressed state, with our right and left brain hemispheres working separately instead of together, therefore denying us full access to our mental faculties. The K27 point is related to the kidney and the left/right brain connectedness.

To help re-establish the left/right connection use crossed wrists: that is, put your left hand on the right side of the body and vice versa. The L14 liver point is related to digestion, both of food and emotions. I've seen a dizzy, nauseous patient recover after a few seconds of massaging here.

Exercise 9: K27 point

Instructions

Crossing wrists, locate tender area underneath collar bone. Massage, while breathing, for a few seconds. Apply firm pressure. Cross wrists the other way and repeat. Tapping firmly is even better.

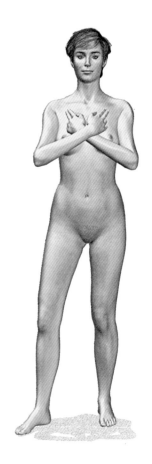

Exercise 10: L14 Point

Instructions

Find a tender spot on the front of the ribcage, underneath the nipple. In a woman, exactly where the underwire of a bra is! Massage or tap firmly in between the ribs for a few seconds. Breathe.

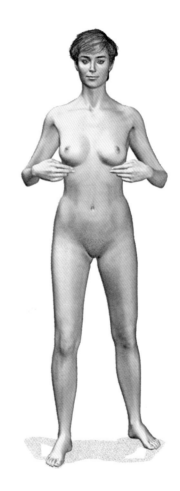

"The dominant force in the whole body is that guiding principle which we term mind or intellect. This is firmly lodged in the mid region of our breast. Here is the place where fear and alarm pulsate. Here is felt the caressing touch of joy. Here then, is the seat of the intellect and mind."
—**Lucretius, On the Nature of Things, Book III (circa 55 BC)**

Chapter 6

Connecting to the Heart Light

THE HEART NEEDS TO pump blood through 15 miles of vascular tubing, not including thousands of miles of tiny capillaries. Scientists have long dropped the 19th century idea of the heart being a simple pump. It has been worked out that if it were, the pressure necessary would require an engine with power sufficient to run a truck to move blood that distance. However, the heart is much more than a muscular organ — it has some very special properties. Biologists noted decades ago that if they cut a heart cell out of a mouse, the cell could beat regularly for a short time, then go into spasm (fibrillation) and die. However, when two separate heart cells started fibrillating and were brought close together, they would somehow interact with each other and both would beat regularly, together, as they would in one heart.

'Somehow, there was an unseen connecting force between those two heart cells that coordinated their beats. In other words, they harmonized.'

Scientists at The Institute of Heartmath (www.heartmath.org) have been measuring the energies put out by heart cells, in terms of EM energy. Our heart, with all the little heart cells communicating and working in synchrony, produces enough energy in each beat to light a small light bulb.

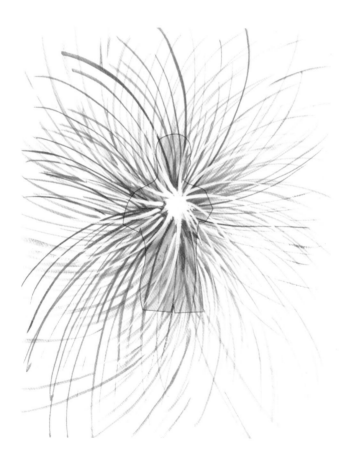

It is this simultaneous emission of electromagnetic energy that builds the biofield, or aura, 12-15 feet around us, with the strongest emissions, or field, close to our bodies. We can really feel this biofield. How often have we felt that someone's been 'in our space' or uncomfortably close at a cash-point machine? A little alarm goes off telling us that a boundary has been breached, that they are dangerously close.

'It seems that at least on a subconscious level, we all know the importance of the heart. Amongst all of the body's organs, it's the heart's qualities that have flowed into our vocabulary: she's got a good heart; heartfelt wishes; get to the heart of the matter, and so on.'

All of the major spiritual traditions emphasize love and the power of the heart. To me, brought up as a Christian, Jesus is a prime example of the power of love.

Since living in Asia I have also connected with Hinduism, Islam and Buddhism, finding very similar energies in these wonderful spiritual traditions.

A glance at ancient world literature immediately shows up many references to the importance of the heart, long regarded as the source of wisdom, courage and love.

HARNESSING THE HEART LIGHT

This simple exercise can be used to connect to your heart light energies, thereby also raising spiritual awareness.

On a more simple level, it's connecting with yourself, a tool to use in times of stress, or when overwhelmed by feelings of hopelessness and despair. Especially when outside events are the cause of your misery, it is useful to turn inside, explore the inner resources, and be pleasantly surprised at what you find.

Exercise 11: Connecting to Heart Light

Instructions

Sitting comfortably (or lying if tired) place both hands on your heart, one on top of the other. On the inhale imagine or feel the light from the heart, like a laser beam, passing up to your neck.

On the exhale, this light runs down your arms into your hands, therefore back to your heart. Feel the subsequent warmth of your hands on your heart.

Keep circulating heart light using the breath in this way.

Heart emotions

Once you get the hang of this, we'll add in an important element: tapping into the heart emotions.

'Emotions are energy in motion.'

While often seeming to overwhelm us, this enormous reserve of energy can be tapped in order to fuel our personal growth. Take time to clarify what each of the four described emotions means to you. These are brief summaries of the four qualities of heart emotion/energy.

Peace

By this I mean the feeling of being truly calm and at one with the world — what the Bible describes as the "peace that passeth". Knowingness that even if a war breaks out around you, it can't affect you as you are completely safe, secure and insulated in your world of peace.

Try to remember a time you felt real peace, perhaps some place in nature — a moment in the mountains or by the beach.

Unconditional Love

If you are a mother, imagine the love you feel for your baby. There will be moments when you know you feel unconditional love, without a doubt, so that whatever your child does or doesn't do wouldn't make any difference to your feelings. If you don't have children, perhaps love of husband, parent, or pet will substitute.

'Unconditional' is the important part. It's easy to love those who love and please us, less easy to love people who annoy or hurt us. As an example, think of Jesus and his examples of unconditional love.

Compassion

'Com' and 'passion' means to be with (another) in pain. This is not feeling sorry for others but more a realization that their plight — illness, loss, earthquake, and so on — could be yours. In that, knowing how you would feel losing your home and family, you form more than a bond with these victims — actually you feel how it must be to be them.

I always think of the master of compassion — Jesus — and have an image of Him with tears rolling down his cheeks.

Compassion is feeling others' suffering as it really is. Not merely sympathizing, but being there for them in their pain, 'holding the space' for them. In that feeling, there comes the realization that as we're all part of the one, not only can we feel their emotions, but that we are them. There's a dissolving of ego boundaries that enables us to transcend our personality self, entering what some would call 'Christ Consciousness'.

Gratitude

Why exactly is gratitude so powerful?

How often have you heard people say, 'It makes you realize how lucky you are'? Perhaps by spending time with handicapped people, or children dying of cancer, there's an instant compassion then recognition of our own blessings. Suddenly we have awareness of the things we've taken for granted and are grateful.

We are so accustomed to focusing on what we haven't got, (let's face it, in a rather self-pitiful way) that when we are grateful for what we have, it seems like we unlock a special energy. It's almost like there's a little pot of gold, or storehouse of lovely energy, waiting for the right key to unlock the treasure chest.

Exercise 12: Increasing the Light of the Heart

Instructions

Try adding emotions to circulating heart light energies. As before (exercise 11), place hands on the heart and circulate heart light. In sequence, take a few seconds focusing on each of the four qualities — unconditional love, peace, compassion, gratitude — feeling the quality radiating from the heart. Really connect to the quality, and feeling.

Spend three breaths on each, continuing to rotate through the qualities. Do these for however long you feel it is appropriate. Feel the difference.

Heart light healing

With practice, you will find it easier and quicker to access the heart energies, or heart space. Some people call this state Christ-Consciousness, meaning that they are feeling, or rather being, the emotions we associate with Christ, such as unconditional love. You can practise using this light energy by placing your hands on some part of your body that doesn't feel so good, for example a sore stomach, or neck.

Exercise 13: Heart Light Healing

Spend a few minutes circulating your heart energies as before. Keeping one hand on your heart, place the other on the relevant part of your body. Continue to circulate heart energy down both arms, then back to your heart.

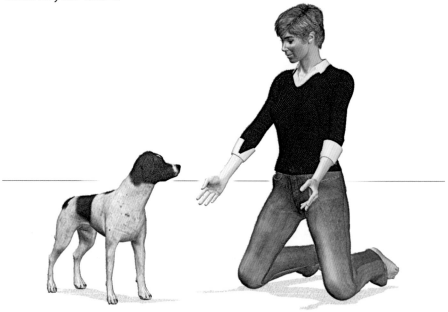

You could also try this with your child or pet (if pets don't want the healing, they'll be quick to move off, so don't force them) by placing a hand on them. They don't need much time — less than a minute. After some practice you'll find it's not necessary to place a hand on your own heart, because you'll automatically direct the heart energy, whether you're touching your body or not.

Separating energy

Especially when working with others, it is very important to ground yourself at the beginning and end. All sorts of complications, such as spacey-ness, or picking up their problems, will otherwise emerge. This is a type of contamination that can occur from simply being around our fellow human beings.

'For example, if you have lunch with a friend who's really angry and bitter, spending every minute complaining about their divorce, how do you feel afterwards?'

So when working with others, it's important to separate your energy from theirs. There are various ways of doing this. One of them is by imagining you're both spotlit in your own individual overhead beam of light. During the healing, each of your spotlights was overlapping with the other's. On finishing, you want to feel you're stepping back so that the two beams no longer overlap, and you're standing in your own, separate light.

"The most beautiful thing we can experience is the mysterious. It is the source of all true art and all science."
—Albert Einstein

Chapter 7

Connection to Universal Light — the Great Mystery

The light of the Earth — Magnetism

A MAGNETIC FIELD IS the energy field between the north and south poles of a magnet. In its most basic energetic form, the Earth is a huge round magnet, radiating an electromagnetic field.

The rotating outer core of the Earth is incredibly hot (about 5,000 degrees centigrade), molten iron, creating the magnetic field all around.

'The Earth's magnetic field is what protects us from harmful radiation from outer space, and has been found to be essential in, for example, the health of astronauts.'

The field is weaker at the North and South poles, which is why solar winds can access our atmosphere to cause the colourful Aurora Borealis — the Northern Lights.

The Earth's magnetic protective effect can be shown in the experiments of Dr Valerie Hunt, who in the 1990s at UCLA studied the effect of eliminating our environmental magnetic field. On removing the EM field from the human volunteers, she found that they became very ill. Their entire neurological system was disturbed, leading to an extreme lack of coordination.

The light of the Sun — Solar flares and winds

It's disguised under the heading 'weather', but the Sun influences our lives much more than we usually imagine. Enormous magnetic lines, 40 times the diameter of the Earth, crash into each other in the Sun's atmosphere, causing phenomena such as Sun spots and the solar wind.

These affect us in different ways — the huge spurts of energy regularly cause havoc with our satellite communication and are dangerous for pilots. Quebec City lost all electricity for nine hours in 1982 when millions of amps overwhelmed the grid, causing huge financial loss and damage.

Since the middle ages, astronomers have noted the relation of sun spots to climate change, such as the 'mini ice age' of the 17th century, when the River Thames in London would regularly freeze over (something not seen in the past few decades). Also, at times of low solar activity, more cosmic rays from outer space will reach the Earth.

The Sun's solar winds travel up to 3 million km per hour, when we can see the effect of their electrically charged particles interacting with Earth's atmosphere in the form of sheets of colour in the sky — the Northern Lights. Usually more visible at the poles, if the solar winds are strong enough they can be seen all over the globe.

Our interaction with these light sources

'We, and all living things, radiate electromagnetic energy.
From the smallest DNA, to cells, to organs, each radiates their own field.
This is our aura, or biofield, as energy psychologists call it.'

In our bodies, contrary to popular belief, more energy is radiated by the heart than the brain. In the shape of a 'torus', or doughnut, the electromagnetic energy arcs out from the heart, reaching 12-15 feet around us. Scientists at the Institute of HeartMath (www.heartmath.org) tell us that the heart's light is much more significant than the brain's.

'According to the same studies, the heart's electromagnetic field
is 5,000 times larger than that of the brain.'

Along the same lines, studies have shown that a foetus, whose heart develops early in life, starts emitting its own EM energy whilst in the womb. It's easy to visualize the foetus's EM field being enveloped by the mother's more powerful one, so by the time it's born, the baby's heart field will be stabilized as it harmonizes with its mother's.

So, both our hearts and the Earth radiate out arcs of electromagnetic energy. On the larger scale, so does the Sun, radiating out to the whole of our solar system.

'Imagine that when the electromagnetic energy of our own hearts
meets with that of the Earth and Sun,
lots of interference patterns are created, each unique.'

To understand these interference patterns, imagine two pebbles dropped in a pond so that a ripple pattern radiates from each one in a circle; the pattern formed where the two sets of waves interact creates a new entity, like an interference pattern. These interference patterns form the world in which we live, and which we manifest. If you think of these overlapping wave patterns as different

"Look deep into Nature, and then you will understand everything better."
—**Albert Einstein**

musical notes, you could say that as humans, sometimes we're harmonizing, and sometimes we're out of tune.

It is interesting to note that the human genome (genetic code) has been found to have 3 billion parts; however, as scientists we only understand the function of about 3% of these. So what do the rest do? A clue can be found in the journal *Science,* which reported in 2001 that DNA had been found to be a superconductor of electricity. Also, we now know that our DNA forms a loop structure. Any electrical engineer knows that electrical current flowing through a loop will produce a magnetic field.

'Knowing that our DNA can both store and radiate EM energy,
perhaps our genes, made up of multiple DNA,
are hard at work interacting with the EM energies of our environment.'

Our DNA are truly mini-lighthouses! So, on a tiny scale there is a magnetic field around our DNA, on a medium scale one round our hearts, and a large one round the Earth and Sun. 'Inductance' is a term used by electrical engineers for the interaction of EM energies. As we know that these magnetic fields interact with each other, it's not too much of a leap to imagine our bodies' EM field reacting, through the process of inductance, with the EM fields of the Earth and Sun.

As this chapter progresses, we'll talk more about these energies, including how to access them. Once we connect to them, they can then be used for healing.

Holographics

The idea of the overlapping energy waves is reminiscent of modern holographic theory:

As before, we need to imagine two pebbles dropped into a pond, causing ripples of concentric, overlapping circles to form in between. This is a type of interference pattern, and a hologram is a 3-D image produced by the interference pattern of two laser (light) beams. The holographic image is the actual interference pattern.

'There are some interesting similarities between holograms and the brain.'

In every part of the hologram, however tiny, the image of the whole is contained. Unlike a standard photograph, any piece is capable of reproducing the whole picture. So, if we divide a holographic picture of a rose in four, when viewed again, each quarter will be a whole rose in its own right.

With stem cell cloning we have recently been introduced to this idea of a small unit developing into a large, sophisticated one. Stem cells are embryonic cells out of which any other type of cell can grow, whether bone, muscle or nerve. They're capable of becoming the whole, full picture.

"As below, so above. As above, so below…"
—Hermetic text

American neurophysiologist Karl Pribram developed his holographic brain theory from study on rats' brains. It had been impossible to understand in which part their memories were held, as even after removing different parts they could still remember complex instructions.

'He postulated that memories were not kept in structures, such as nerves,
but in the impulses that crossed between the nerves,
criss-crossing each other like light laser beams.
This interference pattern was the memory — the hologram.'

This theory explains why we can so quickly retrieve memories — every part of a hologram is connected, or has knowledge of the rest, in a fantastically complex cross-referenced net. For instance, if someone asks us to imagine an orange, we don't have to first file through our A-Z list of fruit to come up with a picture of a round fruit, in the same way as a computer would. We can immediately jump to the correct image.

Secondly, holographic images are non-spatial — i.e. it is possible to superimpose many images in the same space, on the same photographic plate. It's a strange concept, but because the interference patterns and, therefore, the images share the same space, there's an enormous potential for information storage. It's said that one cubic centimetre of the mind can hold up to 10 billion bits of information — the amount in five Encyclopaedia Britannicas!

'Therefore the brain functions like a hologram,
constantly interpreting interference patterns between brain waves.'

This would explain why a certain stimulus, such as a particular smell, can immediately evoke a vivid memory. Our brain doesn't function like a computer in processing enormous lists of stored smell memories and their associations, but jumps immediately to the right one. Also, it seems that the brain selects frequencies from a smorgasbord of holographic interference (that is, energetic information from other people and our surroundings) mathematically transforming them into our sensations and perceptions, when they then become our reality.

'To put it another way,
we choose our perceptions of the world around us to form our reality.'

British physicist David Bohm went a step further in postulating that the Universe itself was a hologram. As we are part of a larger hologram, we all would therefore contain all the information about the whole (that is, the Universe).

I believe that his theory goes a long way to explain puzzling syndromes such as 'idiot savants', the commonly used term for those who are usually mentally impaired, uneducated people whose mathematical calculations can outstrip the fastest computers, or who sometimes with no training become phenomenal musical prodigies.

'According to this theory there would be an inner and outer world,
both mirroring creation in any of its parts... '

"To see the world in a grain of sand
And a heaven in a wild flower
Hold infinity in the palm of your hand
And eternity in an hour."
—**William Blake**

Chapter 8

Connection to Universal Light — the Practical

THE ANCIENT CHINESE (and other indigenous healers over the millennia) had the concept of man being an intermediary between Heaven and Earth. I like this imagery, and love to practise connecting the light of the Earth and Sun, and to draw this energy into and through me. For me, it will balance and heal; through me I feel it can be channelled to heal others. This is my holy Trinity.

When I say 'Heaven', I mean the energy of 'above', whether you call this the energies of God, the Central Sun, the Universe, or 'all that is'.

One of my favourite exercises to connect to this energy is very ancient, and can be seen everywhere from ancient Egyptian hieroglyphics to Qigong practice. This is incredibly useful to help us feel our connection to Heaven and Earth.

'This exercise is thought to stimulate the immune system,
so is good to do at the beginning of a cold or flu.'

Also, it's a good one for healers to do after seeing clients, as any unwanted energies (anger, fear) will flow out of the body. While doing it, remember to visualize your lower hand connecting to the centre of the Earth, upper hand to the Sun. Really feel that you're connecting the two, as a conduit between the light of Heaven and Earth. When your hands come together, imagine you're drawing the light into you. Pushing them apart, you're extending and expanding light out.

At the end, with hands hanging down, really concentrate on connecting with the Earth — here you're grounding your energy. That is, letting your own light energy flow down to merge with, and gain strength from, that of the Earth.

Exercise 14: Connecting the Light of Heaven and Earth

Instructions

Stand with feet apart, knees slightly bent. Hold your hands in front of you, palms facing and try to feel the Qi energy between the two hands. Inhaling, stretch one arm up, one down, wrists bent back. Look up and pause, holding your breath in. Exhaling, bring your hands to the middle, pausing slightly to connect to the Qi energy between them.

have these capable parts, but they're certainly hard to find in times of acute stress.

Spaced out

The opposite of this grounding concept is being spaced out. Think back to the idea of our bodies being vibrating light particles flowing in and out of perception.

If we are going to be truly present in this life, awake and aware, we need to have our total being, including all those little light particles, around us — not on that Thai island where we had a great holiday, with our minds drifting off at every opportunity to sand and sea; not on the unpleasant experience and trauma of an assault we had last year, reliving the experience in moments of fear.

"Be really whole and all things will come to you."
—Lao-Tzu

*'In fact, we usually learn to space out in childhood,
as a way to avoid the reality and discomfort of the present moment.'*

All our energy needs to be in the here and now for us to be effective, and fulfil our purpose in life. If we're 100% together, utilizing all our skills, we are going to find it a lot easier to accomplish and manifest what we desire.

Instructions

While sitting, imagine your energy as being shimmering particles of light all around you, like bright little hummingbirds.

Using your imagination and intention, draw all these particles closer to your body. Use your intention to pull those in that are far away. Feel them as a thick white layer within a few feet of your body.

Harmonizing your body with the Earth's Light

It has been observed that our brain and heart waves synchronize with each other in states of relaxation and meditation. This means that the waves complement each other and are in phase, in the same way that two tuning forks will harmonize.

'It's easy to measure brain waves, which are known to slow down when we sink into deeper meditation states. At around a frequency of 8Hz, they begin to match the Schumann Resonance: this is the measured natural EM frequency vibration of the Earth itself.'